YOUNG PEOPLE'S

YOUNG PEOPLE'S MASS BOOK

The complete Order of Mass
together with the three
Eucharistic Prayers for Children

Edited by Tony Castle
Illustrated by Christa Friend

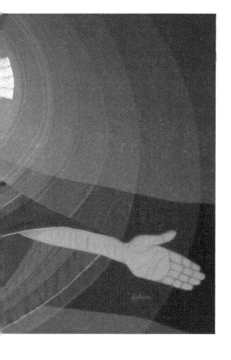

COLLINS

Collins Liturgical Publications
187 Piccadilly, London W1V 9DA

Concordat cum originali: John P. Dewis
Nihil obstat: R. J. Cuming DD
Imprimatur: David Norris VG
Westminster 14 December, 1979

Blue binding   ISBN 0 00 599648 1
White binding   ISBN 0 00 599745 3
Spiral binding   ISBN 0 00 599798 4
First published 1980

Typesetting by Modern Text Typesetting, Southend
Colour origination by Graphic Affairs, Southend
Printed by William Collins Sons & Co Ltd, Glasgow

GIFTS AND GIVING

Playing with your friends and watching television are probably among the things you like doing best. Playing is very different from watching. With friends you join in, you play together, talk together. In front of the T.V. set you just watch! There's no sharing. At Mass we are meant to join in with the other friends of Jesus. If we just watch, it can become boring.

At our birthday celebration, we remember all the things that have happened in our lives, we give presents, we celebrate and share. (Remember, Christmas is a birthday.) The Mass is a celebration—like a party—when gifts are given and people join together to remember God's goodness and love and to thank him for them. The word 'eucharist' (which is often used as a name for the Mass) means 'thanksgiving'.

Do you know what the most wonderful gift ever given was? It was the gift Jesus made of himself to God our Father, when he hung upon the cross. That was a perfect gift, a perfect offering. At Mass, in a very deep and wonderful way, the same gift is offered to God.

We can join in the offering of Jesus. We offer ourselves, along with him, in the bread and the wine. And Jesus himself, through the words and actions of the priest, changes our gifts into his body and blood—just as he did at the last supper. Jesus gives himself to us in the food of life—his body and blood—to help us grow in goodness and love, and to be more like him.

PRAYERS

Prayer of St Francis

Lord, make me an instrument of your peace:
    where there is hatred let me sow love,
    where there is injury let me sow pardon,
    where there is doubt let me sow faith,
    where there is despair let me give hope,
    where there is darkness let me give light,
    where there is sadness let me give joy.
O Divine Master, grant that I may
    not try to be comforted, but to comfort,
    not try to be understood, but to understand,
    not try to be loved, but to love.
Because it is in giving that we receive,
    it is in forgiving that we are forgiven,
    and it is in dying that we are born to eternal life.

Prayer of St Ignatius

Teach us, dear Lord, to serve you as you deserve;
    to give, and not to count the cost;
    to fight and not to heed the wounds;
    to toil and not to seek for rest;
    to labour and not to ask for any reward
    save knowing that we do your holy will.

Lord Jesus,
    I give you my hands to do your work.
    I give you my feet to go your way.
    I give you my eyes to see as you do.
    I give you my tongue to speak your words.
    I give you my mind that you may think in me.
    Above all, I give you my heart that you may love, in
       me, your Father and all mankind.
    I give you my whole self that you may grow in me.
So that it is you, Lord Jesus,
    who live and work and pray in me.

Lancelot Andrewes

Lord,
    I know
    that one of the best ways I can show my love for you
    is by loving other people.
    Sometimes this is easy—
       when I am with people I like.

Please help me when loving is hard,
when people are unkind,
when they don't understand,
when I just don't like them.

Teach me to love as you loved
when you were walking about in Palestine.
Teach me to love as you love now—
    everyone . . .
    always.

Brother Kenneth and
Sister Geraldine

The Order of Mass

COME

Introductory Rites

We sometimes receive invitations to parties—they ask us to come and join others to celebrate. Jesus invites us in each Mass to join him in praising his Father. We celebrate, too, Jesus alive and present among us.

Entry

We come together

As the priest comes in we sing an entrance song or we say the special antiphon for that day.

Greeting

The priest welcomes us

Priest   In the name of the Father, and of the Son, and of the Holy Spirit.

All   **Amen.**

Priest   The grace of our Lord Jesus Christ and the love of God and the fellowship of the Holy Spirit be with you all.

People   **And also with you.**

The priest may use instead one of the following greetings, and then he may say a few words to introduce the Mass.

Priest The grace and peace of God our Father and the Lord Jesus Christ be with you.

People **Blessed be God the Father of our Lord Jesus Christ.**

or

Priest The Lord be with you.

People **And also with you.**

Penitential Rite

We tell God we are sorry

The priest asks us to think of the ways we have hurt God and one another, and to tell God we are sorry.

Priest   My brothers and sisters,
   to prepare ourselves to celebrate the sacred mysteries,
   let us call to mind our sins.

Silence.

All   **I confess to almighty God,**
   and to you, my brothers and sisters,
   that I have sinned through my own fault
   (all strike their breast)
   in my thoughts and in my words,
   in what I have done,
   and in what I have failed to do;
   and I ask blessed Mary, ever virgin,
   all the angels and saints,
   and you, my brothers and sisters,
   to pray for me to the Lord our God.

In place of these words the priest might use one of the following acts of sorrow, or other prayers of the same kind.

Priest   Lord, we have sinned against you:
         Lord, have mercy.
People   **Lord, have mercy.**
Priest   Lord, show us your mercy and love.
People   **And grant us your salvation.**

or

Priest You were sent to heal the contrite:
Lord have mercy.

People **Lord, have mercy.**

Priest You came to call sinners:
Christ have mercy.

People **Christ, have mercy.**

Priest You plead for us at the right hand of the Father:
Lord, have mercy.

People **Lord, have mercy.**

The priest says the prayer of forgiveness

Priest May almighty God have mercy on us,
forgive us our sins,
and bring us to everlasting life.

People **Amen.**

Kyrie

We ask God to keep us in mind

Priest	Lord, have mercy.
People	**Lord, have mercy.**
Priest	Christ, have mercy.
People	**Christ, have mercy.**
Priest	Lord, have mercy.
People	**Lord, have mercy.**

Gloria

We praise and thank God

On most Sundays and on feast days we all sing or say
this song of praise.

All   **Glory to God in the highest,
and peace to his people on earth.**

**Lord God, heavenly King,
almighty God and Father,
we worship you, we give you thanks,
we praise you for your glory.**

**Lord Jesus Christ, only Son of the Father,
Lord God, Lamb of God,
you take away the sin of the world:
have mercy on us;
you are seated at the right hand of the Father:
receive our prayer.**

**For you alone are the Holy One,
you alone are the Lord,
you alone are the Most High,
Jesus Christ,
with the Holy Spirit,
in the glory of God the Father.   Amen.**

Opening Prayer

The priest prays on our behalf

Priest   Let us pray.
Silence. The priest says the special prayer for the day.
We show we agree with it, by saying:

All   **Amen.**

LISTEN

The Liturgy of the Word

*When we love someone,
we like to listen to what
they have to say to us.
The bible tells us of the
wonderful things God
has done for men all
through history. In the
readings, God speaks to
us. We listen to his word.*

First Reading

This is usually from the Old Testament part of the Bible.
It tells us of God's works among men. At the end we say:

Reader   This is the Word of the Lord.
All   **Thanks be to God.**

Responsorial Psalm

In response to the First Reading, a psalm (a hymn or
poem from the Bible) is sung or said. It helps us to give
God praise for the great things he has done for us. We
join in the refrain after each verse.

Second Reading

This is taken from the New Testament, often from the
apostles' letters to the first Christians. At the end we say:

Reader   This is the Word of the Lord.
All   **Thanks be to God.**

14

Gospel Procession and Acclamation

As the Gospel book is carried to the lectern, we show respect for Jesus Christ, who is with us in the Gospel, by standing and singing or saying a verse of welcome.

Gospel Reading

Priest   The Lord be with you.
People   **And also with you.**
Priest   A reading from the holy gospel according to N.
People   **Glory to you, Lord.**

At the end of the Gospel we say:
All   **Praise to you, Lord Jesus Christ.**

Homily   *The priest explains God's words to us*

Profession of Faith

We tell God that we believe in him

We believe in one God,
   the Father, the Almighty,
   maker of heaven and earth,
   of all that is, seen and unseen.

We believe in one Lord, Jesus Christ,
   the only Son of God,
   eternally begotten of the Father,
   God from God, Light from Light,
   true God from true God,
   begotten, not made,
   of one Being with the Father.
   Through him all things were made.
   For us men and for our salvation
      he came down from heaven: All bow
   by the power of the Holy Spirit
   he became incarnate from the Virgin Mary and
        was made man.

For our sake he was crucified under Pontius Pilate;
   he suffered death and was buried.
   On the third day he rose again
      in accordance with the Scriptures;
   he ascended into heaven
      and is seated at the right hand of the Father.
He will come again in glory
      to judge the living and the dead,
   and his kingdom will have no end.

We believe in the Holy Spirit, the Lord, the giver of
    life,
  who proceeds from the Father and the Son.
  With the Father and the Son he is worshipped and
    glorified.
  He has spoken through the Prophets.
  We believe in one holy catholic and apostolic
    Church.
  We acknowledge one baptism for the forgiveness
    of sins.
  We look for the resurrection of the dead,
    and the life of the world to come. Amen.

The Prayer of the Faithful *We pray for God's family*
God's Word to us in the scripture readings, and the act
of faith we have just made together, remind us that we
are part of God's world-wide family. So now we pray
for the needs of that family. We respond, after each
petition, to show we join in the prayer. The priest says a
final prayer, to sum up our petitions, and we all reply:

All **Amen.**

GIVE THANKS

Liturgy of the Eucharist

We show our love by giving gifts, by saying thank you, by doing what is pleasing to the people we love. Now we remember what God has done for us through the life and death of his Son, Jesus. We bring gifts of bread and wine. The priest does what Jesus did at the last supper: he takes the bread and wine, blesses them, breaks the bread, and gives these gifts to us. They become the body which Jesus gave up for us and the blood which he shed for us. When we share them Jesus unites us with himself in his offering of himself to God, our Father.

PREPARATION OF THE GIFTS: TAKING

The gifts are brought up
While the altar is prepared, some of us bring the gifts to the priest. A song may be sung now.

The taking of the gifts
Priest   Blessed are you, Lord, God of all creation.
Through your goodness we have this bread to offer,
which earth has given and human hands have made.
It will become for us the bread of life.
People   **Blessed be God for ever.**
Priest   Blessed are you, Lord, God of all creation.
Through your goodness we have this wine to offer
fruit of the vine and work of human hands.
It will become our spiritual drink.
People   **Blessed be God for ever.**

The priest washes his hands. Then he invites us to pray with him:

Prayer over the Gifts

The priest asks God to accept our gifts

Priest Pray, brethren, that our sacrifice
may be acceptable to God, the almighty Father.

People **May the Lord accept the sacrifice at your hands
for the praise and glory of his name,
for our good, and the good of all his Church.**

The priest says the prayer which is special for this Mass.
We make this prayer ours, too, by saying **'Amen'**

THE EUCHARISTIC PRAYER: BLESSING

In the Eucharistic Prayer, we remember what God has done for us, we praise and thank him for his goodness. Just one Prayer is not enough to say all this in all the ways we want to, so there is a choice of four Prayers which may be used at all Masses (see pp. 21-39). In addition, there are three special Prayers for Masses with young people, which you will find on pp. 46-64.

Dialogue

The priest calls us to prayer

Priest The Lord be with you.
People **And also with you.**
Priest Lift up your hearts.
People **We lift them up to the Lord.**
Priest Let us give thanks to the Lord our God.
People **It is right to give him thanks and praise.**

Preface

The priest says or sings this prayer of thanksgiving. Each season or special day has its own Preface. At the end we all join in:

Sanctus

All **Holy, holy, holy Lord, God of power and might, heaven and earth are full of your glory.**
Hosanna in the highest.

Blessed is he who comes in the name of the Lord.
Hosanna in the highest.

Eucharistic Prayer I

The priest may leave out, if he wishes, the parts in brackets.

We ask God to accept our offering

We come to you, Father,
with praise and thanksgiving,
through Jesus Christ your Son.
Through him we ask you to accept and bless
these gifts we offer you in sacrifice.

We pray for the family of God

We offer them for your holy catholic Church,
watch over it, Lord, and guide it;
grant it peace and unity throughout the world.
We offer them for N. our Pope,
for N. our bishop,
and for all who hold and teach the catholic faith
that comes to us from the apostles.

We pray for those present today

Remember, Lord, your people,
especially those for whom we now pray, N. and N.
Remember all of us gathered here before you.
You know how firmly we believe in you
and dedicate ourselves to you.
We offer you this sacrifice of praise
for ourselves and those who are dear to us.
We pray to you, our living and true God,
for our well-being and redemption.

We honour Mary and the saints

In union with the whole Church
we honour Mary,
the ever-virgin mother of Jesus Christ our Lord
    and God.
We honour Joseph, her husband,
the apostles and martyrs
Peter and Paul, Andrew,
(James, John, Thomas,
James, Philip,
Bartholomew, Matthew, Simon and Jude;
we honour Linus, Cletus, Clement, Sixtus,
Cornelius, Cyprian, Lawrence, Chrysogonus,
John and Paul, Cosmas and Damian)
and all the saints.
May their merits and prayers
gain us your constant help and protection.
(Through Christ our Lord. Amen.)

We ask the Father to accept our gifts

Father, accept this offering
from your whole family.
Grant us your peace in this life,
save us from final damnation,
and count us among those you have chosen.
(Through Christ our Lord. Amen)

Bless and approve our offering;
make it acceptable to you,
an offering in spirit and in truth.
Let it become for us
the body and blood of Jesus Christ,

your only Son, our Lord.

Our gifts become the body and blood of Christ

The day before he suffered
he took bread in his sacred hands
and looking up to heaven,
to you, his almighty Father,
he gave you thanks and praise.
He broke the bread,
gave it to his disciples, and said:

Take this, all of you, and eat it:
this is my body which will be given up for you.

When supper was ended,
he took the cup.
Again he gave you thanks and praise,
gave the cup to his disciples, and said:

Take this, all of you, and drink from it:
this is the cup of my blood,
the blood of the new and everlasting covenant.
It will be shed for you and for all men
so that sins may be forgiven.
Do this in memory of me.

We remember, aloud, what Jesus has done

Priest Let us proclaim the mystery of faith:

People 1 **Christ has died,**
Christ is risen,
Christ will come again.

2 **Dying you destroyed our death,**
rising you restored our life.
Lord Jesus, come in glory.

3 **When we eat this bread and drink this cup,**
we proclaim your death, Lord Jesus,
until you come in glory.

4 **Lord, by your cross and resurrection**
you have set us free.
You are the Saviour of the world.

We call to mind Jesus' death and resurrection

Father, we celebrate the memory of Christ, your Son.
We, your people and your ministers,
recall his passion,
his resurrection from the dead,
and his ascension into glory:
and from the many gifts you have given us
we offer to you, God of glory and majesty,
this holy and perfect sacrifice:
the bread of life
and the cup of eternal salvation.

Look with favour on these offerings
and accept them as once you accepted
the gifts of your servant Abel,
the sacrifice of Abraham, our father in faith,
and the bread and wine offered by your priest
    Melchisedech.
Almighty God,
we pray that your angel may take this sacrifice
to your altar in heaven.
Then, as we receive from this altar
the sacred body and blood of your Son,
let us be filled with every grace and blessing.
(Through Christ our Lord. Amen.)

We remember those who have died

Remember, Lord, those who have died
and have gone before us marked with the sign of faith,
especially those for whom we now pray, N. and N.
May these, and all who sleep in Christ,
find in your presence
light, happiness and peace.
(Through Christ our Lord. Amen.)

We pray for ourselves

For ourselves, too, we ask
some share in the fellowship of your apostles and
    martyrs,
with John the Baptist, Stephen, Matthias, Barnabas,
(Ignatius, Alexander, Marcellinus, Peter,
Felicity, Perpetua, Agatha, Lucy,
Agnes, Cecilia, Anastasia)
and all the saints.

Though we are sinners,
we trust in your mercy and love.
Do not consider what we truly deserve,
but grant us your forgiveness.

Through Christ our Lord
you give us all these gifts.
You fill them with life and goodness,
you bless them and make them holy.

We praise God

Through him,
with him,
in him,
in the unity of the Holy Spirit,
all glory and honour is yours,
almighty Father,
for ever and ever.
All **AMEN.**

Turn to p.40

Eucharistic Prayer II

We ask that the Holy Spirit may bless our gifts
Lord, you are holy indeed,
the fountain of all holiness.
Let your Spirit come upon these gifts to make them
   holy,
so that they may become for us
the body and blood of our Lord, Jesus Christ.

Our gifts become the body and blood of Christ
Before he was given up to death,
a death he freely accepted,
he took bread and gave you thanks.
He broke the bread,
gave it to his disciples, and said:
Take this, all of you, and eat it:
this is my body which will be given up for you.

When supper was ended, he took the cup.
Again he gave you thanks and praise,
gave the cup to his disciples, and said:
Take this, all of you, and drink from it:
this is the cup of my blood,
the blood of the new and everlasting covenant.
It will be shed for you and for all men
so that sins may be forgiven.
Do this in memory of me.

We remember, aloud, what Jesus has done

Priest   Let us proclaim the mystery of faith:

People   1   **Christ has died,**
Christ is risen,
Christ will come again.

2   **Dying you destroyed our death,**
rising you restored our life.
Lord Jesus, come in glory.

3   **When we eat this bread and drink this cup,**
we proclaim your death, Lord Jesus,
until you come in glory.

4   **Lord, by your cross and resurrection**
you have set us free.
You are the Saviour of the world.

We call to mind Jesus' death and resurrection

In memory of his death and resurrection,
we offer you, Father, this life-giving bread,
this saving cup.
We thank you for counting us worthy
to stand in your presence and serve you.
May all of us who share in the body and blood of
    Christ
be brought together in unity by the Holy Spirit.

We pray for God's Church

Lord, remember your Church throughout the world;
make us grow in love,
together with N. our Pope,
N. our bishop, and all the clergy.

We remember those who have died

Remember our brothers and sisters
who have gone to their rest
in the hope of rising again;
bring them and all the departed
into the light of your presence.

We join with the saints in prayer

Have mercy on us all;
make us worthy to share eternal life
with Mary, the virgin mother of God,
with the apostles,
and with all the saints who have done your will
    throughout the ages.
May we praise you in union with them,
and give you glory
through your Son, Jesus Christ.

Through him,   *We praise God*
with him,
in him,
in the unity of the Holy Spirit,
all glory and honour is yours,
almighty Father,
for ever and ever.
All **AMEN.**   Turn to p.40.

Eucharistic Prayer III

We praise God, our Father

Father, you are holy indeed,
and all creation rightly gives you praise.
All life, all holiness comes from you
through your Son, Jesus Christ our Lord,
by the working of the Holy Spirit.
From age to age you gather a people to yourself,
so that from east to west
a perfect offering may be made
to the glory of your name.

We ask that the Holy Spirit may bless our gifts

And so, Father, we bring you these gifts.
We ask you to make them holy by the power of your
    Spirit,
that they may become the body and blood
of your Son, our Lord Jesus Christ,
at whose command we celebrate this eucharist.

Our gifts become the body and blood of Christ

On the night he was betrayed,
he took bread and gave you thanks and praise.
He broke the bread, gave it to his disciples, and said:

Take this, all of you, and eat it:
this is my body which will be given up for you.

When supper was ended, he took the cup.
Again he gave you thanks and praise,
gave the cup to his disciples, and said:
Take this, all of you, and drink from it:
this is the cup of my blood,
the blood of the new and everlasting covenant.
It will be shed for you and for all men
so that sins may be forgiven.
Do this in memory of me.

We remember, aloud, what Jesus has done

Priest   Let us proclaim the mystery of faith:

People   1 **Christ has died,**
           Christ is risen,
           Christ will come again.

          2 **Dying you destroyed our death,**
           rising you restored our life.
           Lord Jesus, come in glory.

          3 **When we eat this bread and drink this cup,**
           we proclaim your death, Lord Jesus,
           until you come in glory.

          4 **Lord, by your cross and resurrection**
           you have set us free.
           You are the Saviour of the world.

We call to mind Jesus' death and resurrection

Father, calling to mind the death your Son endured
   for our salvation,
his glorious resurrection and ascension into heaven,
and ready to greet him when he comes again,
we offer you in thanksgiving this holy and living
   sacrifice.

Look with favour on your Church's offering,
and see the Victim whose death has reconciled us to
   yourself.
Grant that we, who are nourished by his body and
   blood,
may be filled with his Holy Spirit,
and become one body, one spirit in Christ.

May he make us an everlasting gift to you
and enable us to share in the inheritance of your
   saints,
with Mary, the virgin Mother of God;
with the apostles, the martyrs,
(Saint N.—the saint of the day or patron saint) and
   all your saints,
on whose constant intercession we rely for help.

We pray for the people of God

Lord, may this sacrifice,
which has made our peace with you,
advance the peace and salvation of all the world.

Strengthen in faith and love your pilgrim Church on
    earth;
your servant, Pope N., our bishop N.,
and all the bishops,
with the clergy and the entire people your Son has
    gained for you.
Father, hear the prayers of the family you have
    gathered here before you.
In mercy and love unite all your children wherever
    they may be.

We remember those who have died

Welcome into your kingdom our departed brothers
    and sisters,
and all who have left this world in your friendship.
We hope to enjoy for ever the vision of your glory,
through Christ our Lord, from whom all good things
    come.

We praise God

Through him,
with him,
in him,
in the unity of the Holy Spirit,
all glory and honour is yours,
almighty Father,
for ever and ever.
All **AMEN.**

Turn to p.40.

Eucharistic Prayer IV

We praise God for his goodness

Father, we acknowledge your greatness:
all your actions show your wisdom and love.
You formed man in your own likeness
and set him over the whole world
to serve you, his creator,
and to rule over all creatures.
Even when he disobeyed you and lost your friendship
you did not abandon him to the power of death,
but helped all men to seek and find you.
Again and again you offered a covenant to man,
and through the prophets taught him to hope for
    salvation.
Father, you so loved the world
that in the fullness of time you sent your only Son to
    be our Saviour.

He was conceived through the power of the Holy
    Spirit,
and born of the Virgin Mary,
a man like us in all things but sin.
To the poor he proclaimed the good news of
    salvation,
to prisoners, freedom,
and to those in sorrow, joy.
In fulfilment of your will
he gave himself up to death;
but by rising from the dead,
he destroyed death and restored life.

And that we might live no longer for ourselves but
for him,
he sent the Holy Spirit from you, Father,
as his first gift to those who believe,
to complete his work on earth
and bring us the fullness of grace.

We ask that the Holy Spirit may bless our gifts

Father, may this Holy Spirit sanctify these offerings.
Let them become the body and blood of Jesus Christ
our Lord
as we celebrate the great mystery
which he left us as an everlasting covenant.

Our gifts become the body and blood of Christ

He always loved those who were his own in the world.
When the time came for him to be glorified by you,
his heavenly Father,
he showed the depth of his love.

While they were at supper,
he took bread, said the blessing, broke the bread
and gave it to his disciples, saying:
Take this, all of you, and eat it:
this is my body which will be given up for you.

In the same way, he took the cup, filled with wine.
He gave you thanks, and giving the cup to his
disciples, said:
Take this, all of you, and drink from it:
this is the cup of my blood,
the blood of the new and everlasting covenant

It will be shed for you and for all men
so that sins may be forgiven.
Do this in memory of me.

We remember, aloud, what Jesus has done

Priest   Let us proclaim the mystery of faith:
People

1
Christ has died,
Christ is risen,
Christ will come again.

2
Dying you destroyed
   our death,
rising you restored
   our life.
Lord Jesus, come in glory.

3
When we eat this bread
   and drink this cup,
we proclaim your death,
   Lord Jesus,
until you come in glory.

4
Lord, by your cross
   and resurrection
you have set us free.
You are the Saviour
   of the world.

We call to mind Jesus' death and resurrection

Father, we now celebrate this memorial of our
    redemption.
We recall Christ's death, his descent among the dead,
his resurrection, and his ascension to your right hand;
and, looking forward to his coming in glory,
we offer you his body and blood,
the acceptable sacrifice
which brings salvation to the whole world.

We pray for the people of God

Lord, look upon this sacrifice which you have given
    to your Church;
and by your Holy Spirit, gather all who share this
    bread and wine*
into the one body of Christ, a living sacrifice of praise.

Lord, remember those for whom we offer this sacrifice,
especially N. our Pope,
N. our bishop, and bishops and clergy everywhere.
Remember those who take part in this offering,
those here present and all your people,
and all who seek you with a sincere heart.

We remember those who have died

Remember those who have died in the peace of Christ
and all the dead whose faith is known to you alone.

We join with the saints

Father, in your mercy grant also to us your children,
to enter into our heavenly inheritance
in the company of the Virgin Mary, the Mother of God,

*in England and Wales: 'who share this one bread and one cup'.

and your apostles and saints.

Then, in your kingdom, freed from the corruption of sin and death,

we shall sing your glory with every creature through Christ our Lord,

through whom you give us everything that is good.

We praise God

Through him,
with him,
in him,
in the unity of the Holy Spirit,
all glory and honour is yours,
almighty Father,
for ever and ever.

All **AMEN.**

COMMUNION RITE: BREAKING AND GIVING

At a family celebration we join in the games and dancing, we talk to the others there and we all enjoy sharing the party food. At Mass God our Father invites us to take and eat the bread of life, the body and blood of Christ.

The Lord's Prayer

We pray the prayer Jesus taught us
The priest invites us to join him in saying the Lord's Prayer.

Priest   Let us pray with confidence to the Father in the words our Saviour gave us.

All **Our Father, who art in heaven,**
  hallowed be thy name.
  Thy kingdom come.
  Thy will be done on earth, as it is in heaven.
  Give us this day our daily bread,
  and forgive us our trespasses,
  as we forgive those who trespass against us,
  and lead us not into temptation,
  but deliver us from evil.

Priest Deliver us, Lord, from every evil,
  and grant us peace in our day.
  In your mercy keep us free from sin
  and protect us from all anxiety
  as we wait in joyful hope
  for the coming of our Saviour, Jesus Christ.

All **For the kingdom, the power and the glory are**
  yours, now and forever.

Rite of Peace   *We pray for peace*
                    and show our love for each other

Priest Lord Jesus Christ, you said to your apostles:
  I leave you peace, my peace I give you.
  Look not on our sins, but on the faith of your
    Church,
  and grant us the peace and unity of your kingdom
  where you live for ever and ever. *All* **Amen.**

Priest The peace of the Lord be with you always.
People **And also with you.**
Priest Let us offer each other the sign of peace.
  We turn and offer each other the peace of Christ.

The Breaking of Bread

The priest breaks the host, just as Jesus broke the bread at the last supper. Meanwhile, we all sing or say:

Lamb of God, you take away the sins of the world: have mercy on us.

Lamb of God, you take away the sins of the world: have mercy on us.

Lamb of God, you take away the sins of the world: grant us peace.

Communion Procession
We go to receive Christ—our gift from God the Father

The priest prays quietly, to prepare himself to receive the body and blood of Jesus. Then he lifts up the sacred host and calls us to come to communion.

Priest   This is the Lamb of God
who takes away the sins of the world.
Happy are those who are called to his supper.

People   **Lord, I am not worthy to receive you,
but only say the word and I shall be healed.**

A communion song may be sung, or the antiphon of the day recited, as we go to the altar.
Before we receive holy communion, each one of us expresses his faith in the body of Christ:

Priest   The body of Christ.
People   **Amen.**

Silence or Song of Praise
We give thanks in our hearts

There may be a silence after communion. This is a chance for us to say a private 'thank you' to Jesus for coming to us in communion, and for all his loving care of us and of our friends. A song of praise may be sung.

Prayer after Communion
*We pray that our union with Christ
may change our lives*

This prayer varies with each special day or season.
We show our agreement with what it says by replying:

All   **Amen.**

GO

Concluding Rite

'Thank you for having me', we say as we leave a party. At the end of our celebration with Christ we say 'thank you' and we go out to take to others the love we have shared here.

Blessing

The priest blesses us in God's name

Priest The Lord be with you.
People **And also with you.**
Priest May almighty God bless you,
   the Father, and the Son, and the Holy Spirit.
People **Amen.**

Sometimes on special days, there is a longer blessing or a prayer for the people.

Dismissal

We are sent out to live the Mass

Priest Go in the peace of Christ.
or   The Mass is ended, go in peace.
or   Go in peace to love and serve the Lord.
People **Thanks be to God.**

LIVE THE MASS!

We think of God being specially present while we are at Mass, but of course, he's present everywhere. When we go home, he's there; when we go to school, he's there; and when we are out with our friends, he's there too.

Besides finding him in the church and in the words of God in the Bible, there is a special place where God can be found. Not far away, up in heaven, but here, among us. He can be found in people. He is within all the other people you see every day. Not just the ones you like, but everyone. That includes, of course, your brothers and sisters, your parents and teachers too.

Jesus once said something very simple, but very wonderful and very important: 'What you do for anyone else, you do for me.' That means that if we are unkind to a school-mate, we are unkind to Jesus. If we do a good turn for an old person, we do it for Jesus.

We know it's not easy to keep trying to be kind and thoughtful to other people. That's why we need to receive holy communion very often. In communion, Jesus himself comes to give us the help we need. When we try to put others first, we have to make an effort— we have to say 'no' to ourselves—we have to give something of ourselves; it's a kind of offering.

'Living' the Mass means offering ourselves to God, especially by doing what we can to make other people's lives happy; what we do for them we do for Jesus.

Children's Eucharistic Prayers

There's more than one way of saying 'thank you'. We could give a gift, a card, a kiss, or just say something nice. The 'Eucharistic Prayer' is a thank you prayer. The Church has given the three special Eucharistic Prayers that follow, to be used at Masses for children and young people, so that they can offer thanks and praise in their own way.

Eucharistic Prayer for Children I

We thank and praise God for his goodness

Priest   The Lord be with you.

People   **And also with you.**

Priest   Lift up your hearts.

People   **We lift them up to the Lord.**

Priest   Let us give thanks to our Lord our God.

People   **It is right to give him thanks and praise.**

Priest   God our Father,
you have brought us here together
so that we can give you thanks and praise
for all the wonderful things you have done.

We thank you for all that is beautiful in the world
and the happiness you have given us.
We praise you for daylight
and for your word which lights up our minds.
We praise you for the earth,
and all the people who live on it,
and for our life which comes from you.

Priest   We know that you are good.
   You love us and do great things for us.
   (So we all sing (say) together:)

We all join in praise

All   **Holy, holy, holy Lord, God of power and might,
   heaven and earth are full of your glory.
   Hosanna in the highest.**

We thank God for sending Jesus, his Son

Priest Father,
you are always thinking about your people;
you never forget us.
You sent us your Son Jesus,
who gave his life for us
and who came to save us.
He cured sick people;
he cared for those who were poor
and wept with those who were sad.
He forgave sinners
and taught us to forgive each other.
He loved everyone
and showed us how to be kind.
He took children in his arms and blessed them.

We all join in praise

[So we are glad to sing (say):

All **Blessed is he who comes in the name of the Lord.
Hosanna in the highest.**]

We join with the saints in praise

Priest God our Father,
all over the world your people praise you.
So now we pray with the whole Church:
with N., our pope and N., our bishop.
In heaven the blessed Virgin Mary,
the apostles and all the saints
always sing your praise.
Now we join with them and with the angels
to adore you as we sing (say):

We all join in praise

All **Holy, holy, holy Lord, God of power and might,**
heaven and earth are full of your glory.
  Hosanna in the highest.
Blessed is he who comes in the name of the Lord.
  Hosanna in the highest.

We ask that the Holy Spirit may bless our gifts

Priest God our Father,
  you are most holy
  and we want to show you that we are grateful.

  We bring you bread and wine
  and ask you to send your Holy Spirit to make these
    gifts
  the body and blood of Jesus your Son.
  Then we can offer to you
  what you have given to us.

Our gifts become the body and blood of Christ

On the night before he died,
Jesus was having supper with his apostles.
He took bread from the table.
He gave you thanks and praise.
Then he broke the bread, gave it to his friends,
    and said:

Take this, all of you, and eat it:
this is my body which will be given up for you.

Priest   When supper was ended,
  Jesus took the cup that was filled with wine.
  He thanked you, gave it to his friends, and said:

Take this, all of you, and drink from it:
This is the cup of my blood,
the blood of the new and everlasting covenant.
It will be shed for you and for all men
so that sins may be forgiven.
Then he said to them:
Do this in memory of me.

We call to mind Jesus' death and resurrection

We do now what Jesus told us to do.
We remember his death and his resurrection
and we offer you, Father, the bread that gives us life,
and the cup that saves us.
Jesus brings us to you;
welcome us as you welcome him.

We remember, aloud, what Jesus has done

Let us proclaim our faith:

People 1 **Christ has died,**
Christ is risen,
Christ will come again.

2 **Dying you destroyed our death,**
rising you restored our life.
Lord Jesus, come in glory.

3 **When we eat this bread and drink this cup,**
we proclaim your death, Lord Jesus,
until you come in glory.

4 **Lord, by your cross and resurrection**
you have set us free.
You are the Saviour of the world.

We pray for all God's family

Priest Father,
because you love us,
you invite us to come to your table.
Fill us with the joy of the Holy Spirit
as we receive the body and blood of your Son.

Lord,
you never forget any of your children.
We ask you to take care of those we love,
especially of N. and N.,
and we pray for those who have died.

Remember everyone who is suffering from pain or
    sorrow.
Remember Christians everywhere
and all other people in the world.

We are filled with wonder and praise
when we see what you do for us
through Jesus your Son,
and so we sing:

We praise God

Through him,
with him,
in him,
in the unity of the Holy Spirit,
all glory and honour is yours,
almighty Father,
for ever and ever.
All   **AMEN.**

Turn to p.40.

Eucharistic Prayer for Children II

We thank and praise God for his goodness

Priest   The Lord be with you.

People   **And also with you.**

Priest   Lift up your hearts.

People   **We lift them up to the Lord.**

Priest   Let us give thanks to the Lord our God.

People   **It is right to give him thanks and praise.**

Priest   God our loving Father,
we are glad to give you thanks and praise
because you love us.
With Jesus we sing your praise:

All   **Glory to God in the highest.**

or

    Hosanna in the highest.

Priest   Because you love us,
you gave us this great and beautiful world.
With Jesus we sing your praise:

All   **Glory to God in the highest.**

or

    Hosanna in the highest.

Priest   Because you love us,
you sent Jesus your Son
to bring us to you
and to gather us around him
as the children of one family.
With Jesus we sing your praise:

All   **Glory to God in the highest.**

or

    Hosanna in the highest.

Priest For such great love
we thank you with the angels and saints
as they praise you and sing (say):

All **Holy, holy, holy Lord, God of power and might,
heaven and earth are full of your glory.
Hosanna in the highest.
Blessed is he who comes in the name of the Lord.
Hosanna in the highest.**

We thank God for sending Jesus his Son

Priest Blessed be Jesus whom you sent
to be the friend of children and of the poor.
He came to show us
how we can love you, Father,
by loving one another.

Priest   He came to take away sin,
which keeps us from being friends,
and hate, which makes us all unhappy.

He promised to send the Holy Spirit,
to be with us always
so that we can live as your children.

All   **Blessed is he who comes in the name of Lord.
Hosanna in the highest.**

We ask that the Holy Spirit may bless our gifts

Priest   God our Father,
we now ask you
to send your Holy Spirit
to change these gifts of bread and wine
into the body and blood
of Jesus Christ, our Lord.

The night before he died,
Jesus your Son showed us how much you love us.
When he was at supper with his disciples,
he took bread,
and gave you thanks and praise.
Then he broke the bread,
gave it to his friends, and said:

Take this, all of you, and eat it:
this is my body which will be given up for you.

All   **Jesus has given his life for us.**

Priest   When supper was ended,
Jesus took the cup that was filled with wine.
He thanked you, gave it to his friends, and said:

Take this, all of you, and drink from it:
this is the cup of my blood,
the blood of the new and everlasting covenant.
It will be shed for you and for all men
so that sins may be forgiven.

All   **Jesus has given his life for us.**
Priest   Then he said to them:
Do this in memory of me.

We call to mind Jesus' death and resurrection

Priest And so, loving Father,
we remember that Jesus died and rose again
to save the world.
He put himself into our hands,
to be the sacrifice we offer you.

All **We praise you, we bless you, we thank you.**

We pray for God's church

Priest Lord our God,
listen to our prayer.
Send the Holy Spirit
to all of us who share in this meal.
May this Spirit bring us closer together
in the family of the Church,
with N., our pope,
N., our bishop,
all other bishops,
and all who serve your people.

All **We praise you, we bless you, we thank you.**

We pray for all God's family

Priest Remember, Father, our families and friends,
and all those we do not love as we should.
Remember those who have died.
Bring them home to you
to be with you for ever.

All **We praise you, we bless you, we thank you.**

Priest Gather us all together into your kingdom.
There we shall be happy for ever
with the Virgin Mary, Mother of God and our
mother.

There all the friends
of Jesus the Lord
will sing a song of joy.

All **We praise you, we bless you, we thank you.**

We praise God

Priest Through him,
with him,
in him,
in the unity of the Holy Spirit,
all glory and honour is yours,
almighty Father,
for ever and ever.

All **AMEN.**

Turn to p.40.

Eucharistic Prayer for Children III

We praise and thank God for his goodness

Priest	The Lord be with you.
People	**And also with you.**
Priest	Lift up your hearts.
People	**We lift them up to the Lord.**
Priest	Let us give thanks to the Lord our God.
People	**It is right to give him thanks and praise.**
Priest	We thank you,

God our Father.

OUTSIDE THE EASTER SEASON

You made us to live for you and for each other.
We can see and speak to one another,
and become friends,
and share our joys and sorrows.

IN THE EASTER SEASON

You are the living God;
you have called us to share in your life,
and to be happy with you for ever.
You raised up Jesus, your Son,
the first among us to rise from the dead,
and gave him new life.
You have promised to give us new life also,
a life that will never end,
a life with no more anxiety and suffering.

Priest   And so, Father, we gladly thank you
with every one who believes in you;
with the saints and the angels,
we rejoice and praise you, saying:

We all join in praise

All   **Holy, holy, holy Lord, God of power and
might,**
heaven and earth are full of your glory.
Hosanna in the highest.
Blessed is he who comes in the name of the Lord.
Hosanna in the highest.

We thank God for sending Jesus his Son

Priest   Yes, Lord, you are holy;
you are kind to us and to all men.
For this we thank you.
We thank you above all for your Son, Jesus Christ.

OUTSIDE THE EASTER SEASON
You sent him into this world
because people had turned away from you
and no longer loved each other.
He opened our eyes and our hearts
to understand that we are brothers and sisters
and that you are Father of us all.

IN THE EASTER SEASON
He brought us the good news
of life to be lived with you for ever in heaven.
He showed us the way to that life,
the way of love.
He himself has gone that way before us.

He now brings us together to one table
and asks us to do what he did.

We ask God to bless our gifts

Father,
we ask you to bless these gifts of bread and wine
and make them holy.
Change them for us into the body and blood
of Jesus Christ, your Son.

Our gifts become the body and blood of Jesus

On the night before he died for us,
he had supper for the last time with his disciples.
He took bread
and gave you thanks.
He broke the bread
and gave it to his friends, saying:
Take this, all of you, and eat it:
this is my body which will be given up for you.

In the same way he took a cup of wine.
He gave you thanks
and handed the cup to his disciples, saying:
Take this, all of you, and drink from it:
this is the cup of my blood,
the blood of the new and everlasting covenant.
It will be shed for you and for all men
so that sins may be forgiven.

Then he said to them:
Do this in memory of me.

We call to mind Jesus' death and resurrection

God our Father,
we remember with joy
all that Jesus did to save us.
In this holy sacrifice,
which he gave as a gift to his Church,
we remember his death and resurrection.

Father in heaven,
accept us together with your beloved Son.
He willingly died for us,
but you raised him to life again.
We thank you and say:

All **Glory to God in the highest.***

Priest Jesus now lives with you in glory,
but he is also here on earth, among us.
We thank you and say:

All **Glory to God in the highest.**

Priest One day he will come in glory
and in his kingdom
there will be no more suffering,
no more tears, no more sadness.
We thank you and say:

All **Glory to God in the highest.**

We pray for God's family

Priest Father in heaven,
you have called us
to receive the body and blood of Christ at this table
and to be filled with the joy of the Holy Spirit.

*Some other words of praise may be used instead of these.

Through this sacred meal
give us strength to please you more and more.

Lord, our God,
remember N., our pope,
N., our bishop, and all other bishops.

OUTSIDE THE EASTER SEASON
Help all who follow Jesus
to work for peace
and to bring happiness to others.

IN THE EASTER SEASON
Fill all Christians with the gladness of Easter.
Help us to bring this joy
to all who are sorrowful.

Bring us all at last
together with Mary, the Mother of God,
and all the saints,
to live with you
and to be one with Christ in heaven.

We praise God

Through him,
with him,
in him,
in the unity of the Holy Spirit,
all glory and honour is yours,
almighty Father,
for ever and ever.
All **AMEN.**